Testimony
of the
Cross

Project Editor
Grzegorz Gałązka

Meditations and Prayers
Written by Pope John Paul II
For the Stations of the Cross
Held at the Colosseum on Good Friday 2000
© Libreria Editrice Vaticana

Graphics
Giuseppe Sabatelli

English Edition
Liguori Publications 2002
Liguori, Missouri

ISBN 0-7648-0882-6
Library of Congress Catalog Control Number: 2001099271

Printed in Italy
06 05   5 4

Testimony
of the
Cross

Meditations and Prayers
of His Holiness Pope John Paul II
For the Stations of the Cross at the Colosseum
Good Friday 2000

Photographs by
Grzegorz Gałązka

Liguori
LIGUORI, MISSOURI

Extraordinary Testimony of the Cross

"A magnificent and terrible image will last forever: a very old man, exhausted, practically in tears, observing the sacred icon at the feet of the Crucified, in a gesture of humility unmatched for centuries, presenting himself thus as the contemporary of his whole institution: the poor, the persecuted of every place and time...," writes Giuseppe De Carli, in his introduction to the book, *The Grand Jubilee: Images and Words*, commenting on the "Day of Forgiveness," on March 12, 2000, when John Paul II asked Christ to pardon the sins committed by Christians during the past two thousand years.

The Holy Father John Paul II, over the course of his life, has encountered the Cross in an exceptional way: He has experienced it from Nazism and Communism in Poland, through the assassination attempt on his own life, through sickness and the weight of advanced age.

At Fatima on May 12, 2000, Cardinal Angelo Sodano, in presenting the "third secret of Fatima," noted that "the bishop dressed in white" [who appears in this communication and] who prays for all the faithful is the Pope. He, too, laboriously making his way toward the Cross through the heaps of corpses of the tortured victims (bishops, priests, religious, nuns, and many lay people), falls to the earth as if dead, beneath the blows of firearms.

In this volume, the photographs of Grzegorz Gałązka express the mystery of the Cross in John Paul II's life with a language that mere words could not express. The text, written personally by the Pope for the Stations of the Cross held at the Colosseum on Good Friday of the year 2000, expresses the richness of his spirituality, as a testimony to the Cross, to Faith, to Life, and to Love.

On Calvary we contemplate a love whose full complement is the gift of one's life; but at the same time and for this very reason it becomes a symbol that challenges and disturbs consciences. "As we celebrate the Passion of the Lord and take part in the Via Crucis, we cannot forget the power of this love which gives itself without measure," said John Paul II on April 11, 2001.

"We wish to profess," he continues, "that, through his Cross, the Son of God, in accepting this humiliation, has opened to humanity the path to glory....Let this truth be for us the light and power of this new millennium....Ave, Crux! Hail, through all the years and centuries of this new time that now opens up before us!"

"If any want
to become my followers,
let them deny themselves
and take up their cross
and follow me."
(Mt 16:24)

The Stations of the Cross

Meditations and Prayers by the Holy Father John Paul II

OPENING PRAYER

The Holy Father: In the name of the Father, and of the Son, and of the Holy Spirit.
R/. Amen.

"If any man would come after me, let him deny himself and take up his cross and follow me" (Mt 16:24).

Good Friday evening.
For twenty centuries,
the Church has gathered on this evening
to remember and to re-live
the events of the final stage
of the earthly journey of the Son of God.
Once again this year,
the Church in Rome
meets at the Colosseum,
to follow in the footsteps of Jesus,
who "went out, carrying his cross,
to what is called the place of the skull,
which is called in Hebrew Golgotha" (Jn 19:17).

We are here because we are convinced that
the Way of the Cross of the Son of God
was not simply a journey
to the place of execution.
We believe that every step of the Condemned
Christ, every action and every word,
as well as everything felt and done
by those who took part in this tragic drama,
continues to speak to us.
Through his suffering and death,
Christ also reveals to us the truth about
God and man.
In these pages
we want to concentrate
on the full meaning of that event,
so that what happened may speak with

new power to our minds and hearts,
and become the source of grace
to truly share in it.
To share means to have a part.
What does it mean to have a part
in the Cross of Christ?
It means to experience, in the Holy Spirit,
the love hidden within the Cross of Christ.
It means to recognize, in the light of this love,
our own cross.
It means to take up that cross once more and,
strengthened by this love, to continue our journey...

To journey through life,
in imitation of the one who "endured the cross,
despising the shame, and is seated at
the right hand of the throne of God" (Heb 12:2).

BRIEF PAUSE FOR SILENCE.

Let us pray
Lord Jesus Christ,
fill our hearts with the light of your Spirit,
so that by following you on your final journey
we may come to know the price of our
Redemption and become worthy of a share
in the fruits of your Passion, Death and
Resurrection.
You who live and reign forever and ever.
R/. Amen.

First Station
Jesus Is Condemned to Death

V/. We adore you, O Christ, and we bless you.
R/. Because by your holy Cross you have redeemed the world.

"Are you the King of the Jews?" (Jn 18:33).
"My Kingdom is not of this world; if my Kingdom were of this world, my servants would fight, that I might not be handed over to the Jews; but my Kingdom is not from the world" (Jn 18:36).
Pilate said to him:
"So you are a king?"
Jesus answered:
"You say that I am a king. For this I was born, and for this I have come into the world, to bear witness to the truth. Everyone who is of the truth hears my voice."
Pilate said in answer:
"What is truth?"

At this point, the Roman Procurator saw no need for further questions. He went to the Jews and told them: "I find no crime in him" (see Jn 18:37–38).

The tragedy of Pilate is hidden in the question: What is truth? This was no philosophical question about the nature of truth, but an existential question about *his own relationship with truth*. It was an attempt to escape from the voice of conscience, which was pressing him to acknowledge the truth and follow it. When people refuse to be guided by truth, ultimately, they are ready to even condemn an innocent person to death.
The accusers sense this weakness in Pilate and so they do not yield. They relentlessly call for Jesus' death by crucifixion. Pilate's attempts at half measures are of no avail. The cruel punishment of scourging that is inflicted upon the Accused is not enough. When the Procurator brings Jesus, scourged and crowned with thorns, before the crowd, he seems to be looking for words which he thinks might soften the intransigence of the mob.
Pointing to Jesus he says: *Ecce homo!* Behold the man!

But the answer comes back: "Crucify him, crucify him!" Pilate then tries to buy time: "Take him yourselves and crucify him, for I find no crime in him" (Jn 19:5—7).

Pilate is increasingly convinced that the Accused is innocent, but this is not enough for him to decide in his favor.
The accusers use their final argument: "If you release this man, you are no friend of Caesar; everyone who makes himself a king sets himself against Caesar" (Jn 19:12).
This argument is clearly a threat. Recognizing the danger, Pilate finally gives in and pronounces the sentence. But not without the contemptuous gesture of washing his hands: "I am innocent of this...blood; see to it yourselves!" (Mt 27:24).
Thus was Jesus, the Son of the living God, the Redeemer of the world, condemned to death by crucifixion.

Over the centuries the denial of truth has spawned suffering and death. It is the innocent who pay the price of human hypocrisy.
Half measures are never enough. Nor is it enough to wash one's hands. Responsibility for the blood of the righteous remains.

This is why Christ prayed so fervently for his disciples in every age: Father, "Sanctify them in the truth; your word is truth" (Jn 17:17).

PRAYER
Lord Jesus Christ, you accepted an unjust judgment.
Grant to us and to all the men and women of our time
the grace to remain faithful to the truth.
Do not allow the weight of responsibility
for the sufferings of the innocent
to fall upon us and upon those who come after us.
To you, O Jesus, just Judge,
honor and glory forever and ever.
R/. Amen.

All:
Our Father who art in heaven,
hallowed be thy name,
thy kingdom come,
thy will be done, on earth as it is in heaven.
Give us this day our daily bread,
and forgive us our trespasses
as we forgive those who trespass against us.
Lead us not into temptation,
but deliver us from evil.
R/. Amen.

Stabat Mater
At the Cross her station keeping
stood the mournful Mother weeping,
close to Jesus to the last.

Second Station
Jesus Takes Up His Cross

V/. We adore you, O Christ, and we bless you.
R/. Because by your holy Cross you have redeemed the world.

The cross. The instrument of a shameful death. It was not lawful to condemn a Roman citizen to death by crucifixion: it was too humiliating. The moment that Jesus of Nazareth took up the Cross in order to carry it to Calvary marked a turning point in the history of the cross.
The symbol of a shameful death, reserved for the lowest classes, the cross *becomes a key*. From now on, with the help of this key, humanity will open the door to the deepest mystery of God. Through Christ's acceptance of the Cross, the instrument of his own self-emptying, all people will come to know that *God is love*.

Love without limitations: "God so loved the world that he gave his only Son, that whoever believes in him should not perish but have eternal life" (Jn 3:16).

This truth about God was revealed in the Cross.
Could it not have been revealed in some other way?
Perhaps. But God *chose the Cross*.
The Father chose the Cross for his Son, and his Son shouldered it, carried it to Mount Calvary and on it, offered his life.
"In the Cross there is suffering, in the Cross there is salvation, in the Cross there is a lesson of love.
O God, he who once has understood you, desires nothing else, seeks nothing else."
Polish Lenten Hymn

The Cross is the sign of a love without limits!

PRAYER
Lord Jesus Christ, who accepted the Cross at the hands of men in order to make of it a sign of God's saving love for humanity, grant us and all the men and women of our time the grace of faith in this infinite love.
By passing on to the new millennium the sign of the Cross, may we be authentic witnesses to the Redemption.
To you, O Jesus, Priest and Victim, praise and glory forever.
R/. Amen.

All: *Our Father...*

Stabat Mater
Through her heart, his sorrow sharing, all his bitter anguish bearing, now at length the sword had passed.

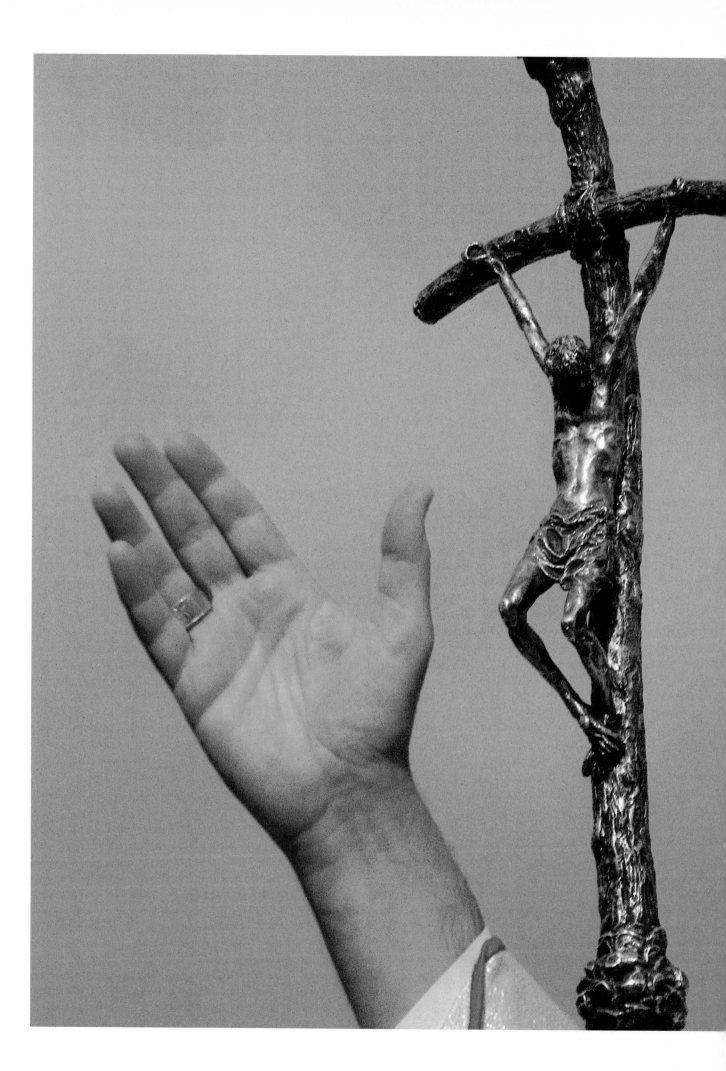

Third Station
Jesus Falls for the First Time

V/. We adore you, O Christ, and we bless you.
R/. Because by your holy Cross you have redeemed the world.

"God laid on him the sins of us all" (*see* Isa 53:6).
"All we like sheep have gone astray;
we have turned every one to his own way;
and the Lord has laid on him
the iniquity of us all" (Isa 53:6).

Jesus falls under the Cross. This will happen three times along the comparatively short stretch of the "via dolorosa."
Exhaustion makes him fall. His body is stained with blood from the scourging, his head is crowned with thorns. All this causes his strength to fail.
So he falls, and the weight of the Cross crushes him to the ground.

We must go back to the words of the Prophet, who had foreseen this fall centuries earlier. It is as though he were contemplating it with his own eyes: seeing the Servant of the Lord, on the ground under the weight of the Cross, he tells us the real cause of his fall. It is this: "*God laid on him the sins of us all.*"
It was our sins that crushed the divine Condemned One to the ground.
It was our sins that determined the weight of the Cross that he carries on his shoulders.
It was our sins that made him fall.

With difficulty, Christ gets up again to continue his journey.
The soldiers escorting him urge him on with shouts and blows.
After a moment the procession sets out again.

Jesus falls and gets up again.
In this way, the Redeemer of the world addresses in a wordless way all those who fall.
He exhorts them to get up again.
"He himself bore our sins in

his body on the wood of the cross, that we might no longer live for sin but for righteousness—by his wounds we have been healed" (*see* 1 Pt 2:24).

PRAYER
O Christ, as you fall under the weight of our faults and rise again for our redemption,
we pray, help us and all those who are weighed down by sin to stand up again
and continue the journey.
Give us the strength of the Spirit to carry, with you, the cross of our weakness.
To you, O Jesus, crushed under the weight of our faults, be our praise and love forever.
R/. Amen.

All: *Our Father...*

Stabat Mater
Oh, how sad and sore distressed
was that Mother highly blessed
of the sole begotten One!

Fourth Station
Jesus Meets His Mother

V/. We adore you, O Christ, and we bless you.
R/. Because by your holy Cross you have redeemed the world.

"Do not be afraid, Mary, for you have found favor with God. And behold, you will conceive in your womb and bear a son, and you shall call his name Jesus. He will be great, and will be called the Son of the Most High; and the Lord God will give to him the throne of his father David, and he will reign over the house of Jacob forever; and his kingdom will have no end" (Lk 1:30–33).

Mary remembered these words. She often returned to them in the secret of her heart. When she met her Son on the way of the

Cross, perhaps these very words came to her mind with particular force. "He will reign...His kingdom will have no end," the heavenly messenger had said.

Now, as she watches her Son, who was condemned to death, carrying the Cross on which he must die, she might ask herself, in a very human way: So how can these words be fulfilled? In what way will he reign over the House of David? And how can it be that his kingdom will have no end? Humanly speaking, these are reasonable questions.

But Mary remembered, when she first heard the angel's message, she had replied: "Behold, I am the handmaid of the Lord. May it be done to me according to your word" (Lk 1:38).

Now she sees that her word is being fulfilled as the *word of the Cross*. Because she is a mother, Mary suffers deeply.

But she answers now as she had answered then, at the Annunciation: *"May it be done to me according to your word."*

In this way, as any mother would, she embraces both the cross as well as the divine Condemned One.

On the way of the Cross, Mary shows herself to be the Mother of the Redeemer of the world.

"All you who pass by the way, look and see whether there is any suffering like my suffering, which has been dealt me" (Lam 1:12).

It is the Sorrowful Mother who speaks,
the Handmaid who is obedient to the last,
the Mother of the Redeemer of the world.

PRAYER

O Mary, who walked
the way of the Cross with your Son,
your mother's heart torn by grief,
but mindful always of your *fiat*
and fully confident that He to whom nothing is impossible
would be able to fulfill his promises,
implore for us and for the generations yet to come
the grace of surrender to God's love.
Help us, in the face of suffering, rejection, and trials,
however prolonged and severe,
never to doubt his love.
To Jesus, your Son,
honor and glory forever and ever.
R/. Amen.

All: *Our Father...*

Stabat Mater
Christ above in torment hangs,
she beneath beholds the pangs
of her dying, glorious Son.

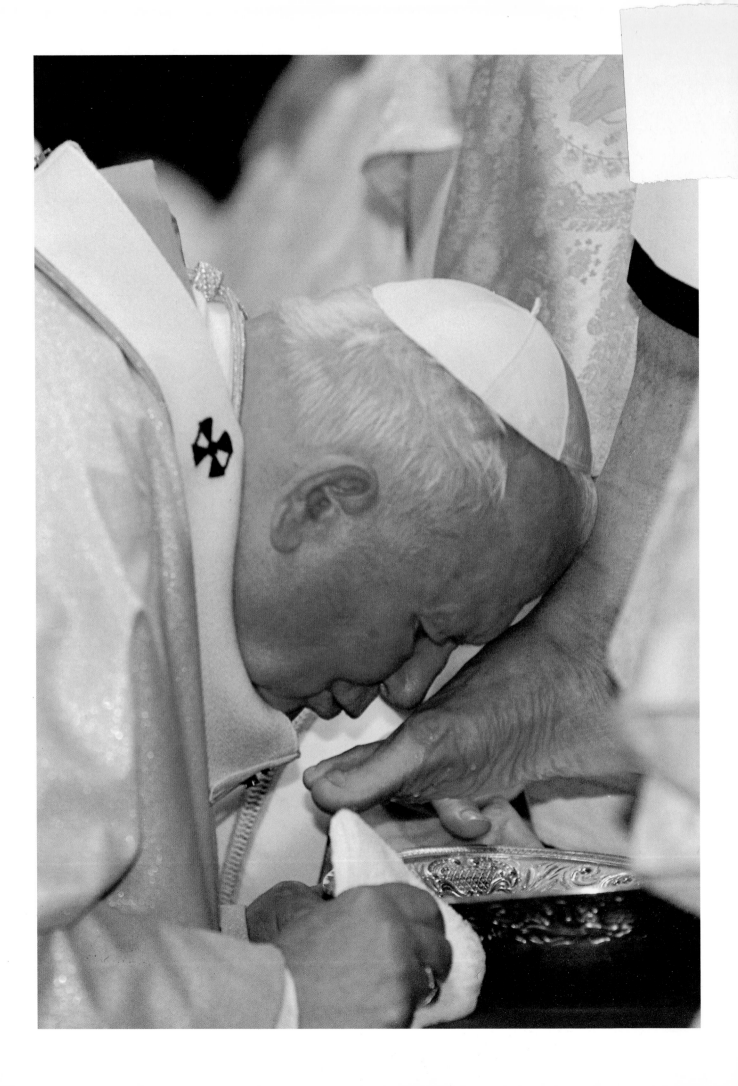

Fifth Station
Simon of Cyrene Helps Jesus to Carry His Cross

V/. We adore you, O Christ, and we bless you.

R/. Because by your holy Cross you have redeemed the world.

They compelled Simon (see Mk 15:21).
The Roman soldiers did this because they feared that, in his exhaustion, the Condemned Man would not be able to carry the Cross as far as Golgotha. Then they would not be able to carry out the sentence of crucifixion.
They were looking for someone to help carry the Cross.
Their eyes fell on Simon. They compelled him to take the weight upon his shoulders. We can imagine that Simon did not want to do this and objected. Carrying the cross together with a convict could be considered as an act offensive to the dignity of a free man.

Although he was unwilling, Simon took up the Cross to help Jesus.

In a Lenten hymn, we hear the words: "Under the weight of the Cross, Jesus

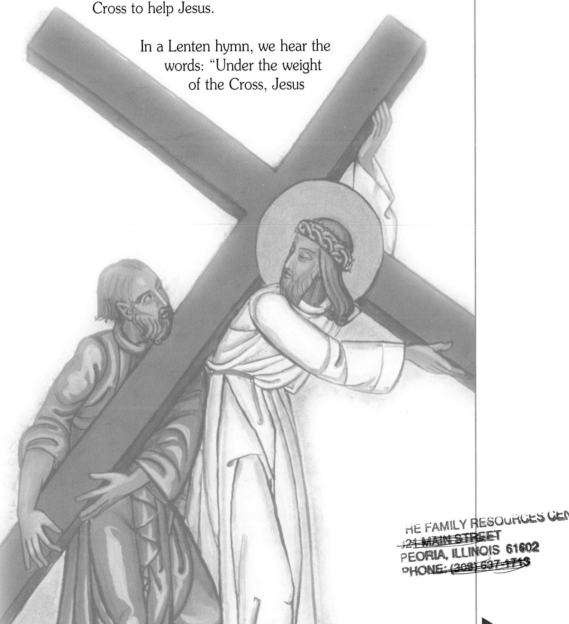

▶

welcomes the Cyrenean." These words allow us to discern a total change of perspective: the divine Condemned One is someone who, in a certain sense, *"makes a gift" of his Cross.*
Was it not he who said: "He who does not take up his cross and follow me is not worthy of me" (Mt 10:38)?
Simon receives a gift.
He has become "worthy" of it.
What the crowd might see as an offense to his dignity has, from the perspective of redemption, given Simon a new dignity.
In a unique way, the Son of God has made him a sharer in his work of salvation.

Is Simon aware of this?
The evangelist Mark identifies Simon of Cyrene as "the father of Alexander and Rufus" (15:21).
If the sons of Simon of Cyrene were known to the first Christian community, it can be presumed that Simon, too, while carrying the Cross, came to believe in Christ. At first forced to participate, he came to freely accept his participation in salvation history. It seems that he was deeply touched by the words: "and whoever does not take up the cross and follow me is not worthy of me" (Mt 10:38).

By his carrying of the Cross, *Simon was brought to the knowledge of the gospel of the Cross.*

Since then, this gospel has spoken to many, countless Cyreneans called in the course of history to carry the cross with Jesus.

PRAYER
O Christ, you gave to Simon of Cyrene
the dignity of carrying your Cross.
Welcome us too under its weight,
welcome all men and women
and grant to everyone the gift of readiness to serve.
Do not allow us to turn away from those
who are crushed by the cross of illness
loneliness, hunger or injustice.
As we carry each other's burdens,
help us to become witnesses to the gospel of the Cross
and witnesses to you,
who live and reign forever and ever.
R/. Amen.

All: *Our Father...*

Stabat Mater
Is there one who would not weep,
overwhelmed in miseries so deep,
Christ's dear Mother to behold?

Sixth Station
Veronica Wipes the Face of Jesus

V/. We adore you, O Christ, and we bless you.
R/. Because by your holy Cross you have redeemed the world.

Veronica does not appear in the Gospels. Her name is not mentioned, even though the names of other women who accompanied Jesus do appear.

It is possible, therefore, that the name refers more to what the woman did. In fact, according to tradition, on the road to Calvary, a woman pushed her way through the soldiers escorting Jesus and, with a veil, wiped the sweat and blood from the Lord's face. That face remained imprinted on the veil, a faithful reflection, a *"true icon."* This would be the reason for the name Veronica, which means "true icon." If this is so, the name which evokes the memory of what this woman did carries with it the deepest *truth about her.*

One day, Jesus drew the criticism of onlookers when he defended a sinful woman who had poured perfumed oil on his feet and dried them with her hair. To those who objected, he replied: "Why do you trouble this woman? For she has done a beautiful thing to me....In pouring this ointment on my body she has done it to prepare me for burial" (Mt 26:10, 12).

These words, likewise, could be applied to Veronica.

Thus we see the profound eloquence of this event. The Redeemer of the world presents Veronica with an authentic image of his face.

The veil upon which the face of Christ remains imprinted becomes a message for us.

In a certain sense it says: This is how every act of goodness, every gesture of true love towards one's neighbor, strengthens the likeness of the Redeemer of the world in the one who acts that way.

Acts of love do not pass away. Every act of goodness, of understanding, and of service leaves, on our hearts, an indelible imprint, and makes us ever more like the One who "emptied himself, taking the form of a servant" (Phil 2:7). This is what shapes our identity and gives us our true name.

PRAYER

Lord Jesus Christ,
you accepted a woman's selfless gesture of love,
and in exchange ordained that future generations
should remember her by the name that reflects
what she did.

Grant that our works and the works of all who will
come after us make us more like you and will
leave in the world the reflection of your infinite
love.

To you, O Jesus, splendor of the Father's glory,
praise and glory forever.
R/. Amen.

All: *Our Father...*

Stabat Mater
Can the human heart refrain
from partaking in her pain,
in that Mother's untold pain?

Seventh Station
Jesus Falls for the Second Time

V/. We adore you, O Christ, and we bless you.

R/. Because by your holy Cross you have redeemed the world.

"I am a worm, and no man; scorned by men, and despised by the people" (Ps 22:6).

These words of the Psalm come to mind as we see Jesus fall to the ground a second time under the weight of the Cross.

Here, in the dust of the earth, lies the Condemned One, crushed by the weight of his Cross. His strength diminishes, draining away, bit by bit. But, with great effort, he gets up again, continuing on his way.

To us sinners, what does this second fall say? More than the first one, it seems to urge us to get up, *to get up again* on our way of the cross.

Cyprian Norwid wrote: "Not behind us with the Savior's Cross, but behind the Savior with our own Cross." A brief saying, but one that conveys a great deal of truth. It explains how Christianity is the religion of the Cross. It tells us that every person on earth meets Christ, who carries the Cross and falls under its weight.

In his turn, Christ, on the way to Calvary, meets every man and woman and, falling under the weight of the Cross, he does not cease to proclaim the Good News.

For two thousand years, the gospel of the Cross has spoken to us.
For twenty centuries, Christ gets up again from his fall, and meets those who fall.
Throughout these two millennia, many people have learned that falling does not mean the end of the road.
In meeting the Savior, they hear his reassuring words: "My grace is sufficient for you; for my power is made perfect in weakness" (2 Cor 12:9).
Comforted, they get up again and bring to the world, the word of *hope which comes from the Cross*.

Today, having crossed the threshold of the new millennium, we are called to delve more deeply into the meaning of this encounter.
Our generation must pass, to future centuries, the Good News that we are lifted up, again, in Christ.

PRAYER

Lord Jesus Christ,
you fall under the weight of human sin
and you get up again in order to take our sins upon yourself and cancel them.
Give to us, weak men and women,
the strength to carry the cross of daily life
and to get up again from our falls,
so that we may bring, to future generations,
the Gospel of your saving power.
To you, O Jesus, our support when we are weak,
praise and glory forever.
R/. Amen.

All: *Our Father...*

Stabat Mater
Bruised, derided, cursed, defiled,
she beheld her tender Child,
all with bloody scourges rent.

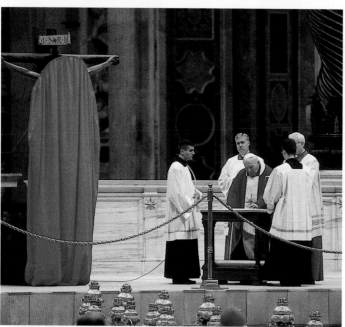

Eighth Station
Jesus Speaks to the Women of Jerusalem

V/. We adore you, O Christ, and we bless you.

R/. Because by your holy Cross you have redeemed the world.

"Daughters of Jerusalem, do not weep for me,
but weep for yourselves and for your children.
For behold, the days are coming when they will say,
'Blessed are the barren, and the wombs that never bore,
and the breasts that never gave suck!'
Then they will begin to say to the mountains,
'Fall on us'; and to the hills, 'Cover us.'

For if they do this when the wood is green, what will happen when it is dry?" (Lk 23:28–31).

These are the words of Jesus to the women of Jerusalem who were weeping with compassion for the Condemned One.

"Do not weep for me, but weep for yourselves and for your children." At the time, it was certainly difficult to understand the meaning of these words; however they contained a prophecy that would soon come to pass. Shortly before, Jesus had wept over Jerusalem, foretelling the terrible fate that awaited the city.

Now he seems to be referring, again, to that fate: "but weep for your children...." Weep, because these, your very children, will be witnesses and share in the destruction of Jerusalem, the Jerusalem which *did not know the time of her visitation*" (see Lk 19:44).

If, as we follow Christ on the way of the Cross, our hearts are moved with pity for his suffering, we cannot forget that admonition.

"For if they do this when the wood is green, what will happen when it is dry?" For our generation, which has just left a millennium behind, rather than weep for Christ crucified, now is the moment for us to recognize "*the time of our visitation.*" The dawn of the resurrection is already shining forth. "Behold, now is the acceptable time; behold, now is the day of salvation" (2 Cor 6:2).

To each of us Christ addresses these words of the book of Revelation: "Behold, I stand at the door and knock; if any one hears my voice and opens the door, I will come in to him and eat with him, and he with me. He who conquers, I will grant him to sit with me on my throne, as I myself conquered and sat down with my Father on his throne" (Rev 3:20–21).

PRAYER

O Christ, you came into this world
to visit all those who await salvation.
Grant that our generation
will recognize the time of its visitation
and share in the fruits of your redemption.
Do not permit that there should be weeping for us
and for the men and women of the new century
because we have rejected our merciful Father's outstretched hand.
To you, O Jesus, born of the Virgin Daughter of Zion,
be honor and praise forever and ever.
R/. Amen.

All: *Our Father...*

Stabat Mater
Let me share with you his pain
who for all my sin was slain,
who for me in torments died.

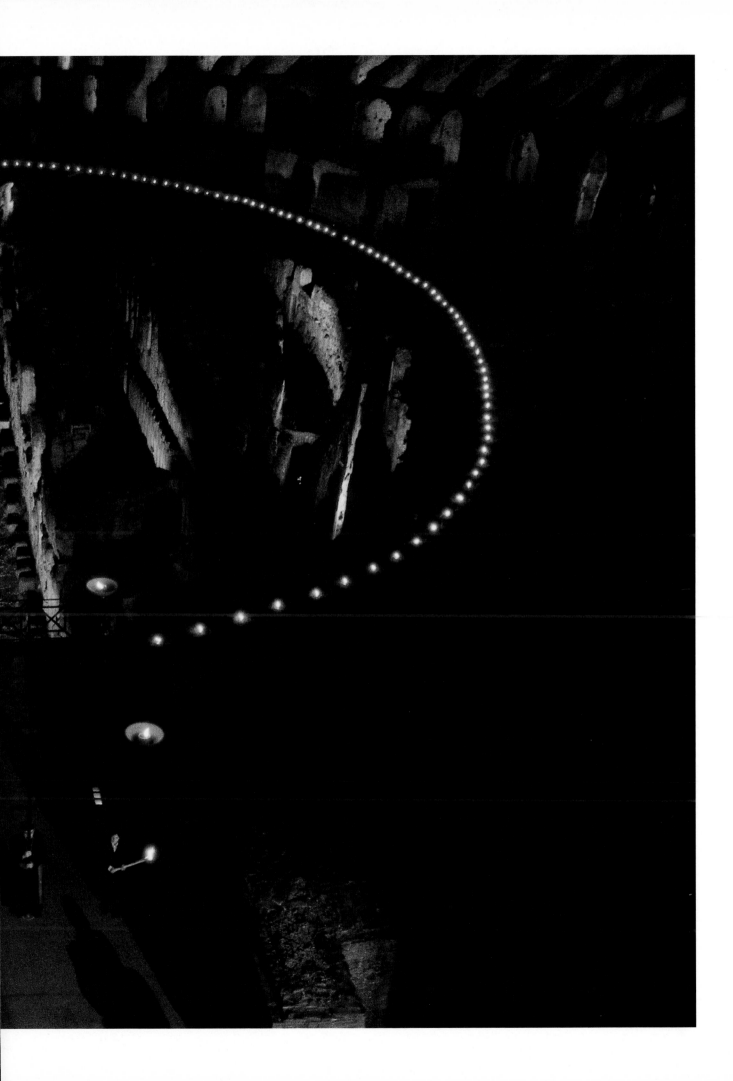

Ninth Station
Jesus Falls the Third Time

V/. We adore you, O Christ, and we bless you.
R/. Because by your holy Cross you have redeemed the world.

Once more, Christ has fallen to the ground under the weight of the Cross. The crowd watches, wondering whether he will have the strength to rise again.

Saint Paul writes: "Though he was in the form of God, he did not count equality with God a thing to be grasped, but emptied himself taking the form of a servant, being born in human likeness. And being found in human form, he humbled himself and became obedient unto death, even death on a Cross" (Phil 2:6–8).
The third fall seems to express just this: *the self-emptying, the kenosis of the Son of God,* his humiliation beneath the Cross.
Jesus had said to the disciples that he had come not to be served but to serve (see Mt 20:28).
In the Upper Room, bending low to the ground and washing their feet, he sought, as it were, to prepare them for his humiliation.
Falling to the ground for the third time on the way of the Cross, *he cries out loudly to us, once more, of the mystery of himself.*

This Condemned Man, crushed to the ground beneath the weight of the Cross, now very near the place of punishment, tells us: "I am the way, and the truth and the life" (Jn 14:6).
"He who follows me will not walk in darkness, but will have the light of life" (Jn 8:12).
Let us not be dismayed by the sight of a condemned man who falls to the ground exhausted under the cross.
Within this outward sign of his approaching death, the light of life lies hidden.

PRAYER
Lord Jesus Christ,
through your humiliation beneath the Cross you revealed to the world the price of its redemption.
Grant to the men and women of the third millennium the light of faith, so that, as they recognize in you, the Suffering Servant of God and man, they may have the courage to follow the same path which, by way of the Cross and self-emptying, leads to life without end.
To you, O Jesus, our support when we are weak, be honor and glory forever.
R/. Amen.

All: *Our Father...*

Stabat Mater
O you Mother, fount of love!
Touch my spirit from above,
make my heart with yours accord.

Tenth Station
Jesus Is Stripped and Offered Gall and Vinegar to Drink

V/. We adore you, O Christ, and we bless you.
R/. Because by your holy Cross you have redeemed the world.

"…when he tasted it, he would not drink it" (Mt 27:34).
He did not want a sedative, which would have dulled his awareness during the agony.
He wanted *to be fully aware as he suffered on the Cross*, accomplishing the mission he had received from the Father.

That was not what the soldiers who were in charge of the execution were accustomed to seeing. Since they had to nail the condemned man to the Cross, they tried to dull his senses and his consciousness.

But with Christ this could not be. Jesus knows that his death on the Cross must be a sacrifice of expiation.
This is why he wants to remain alert, right to the very end.
Without being fully conscious, he could not, in complete freedom, accept the *full measure of suffering.*

Behold, he must mount the Cross in order to offer the sacrifice of the New Covenant.

He is the Priest. By means of his own blood, he must enter the eternal dwelling places, having accomplished the world's redemption (see Heb 9:12).

Conscience and freedom: these are the essential elements of a fully human action.
The world has so many ways to weaken our will and darken our conscience.
They must be carefully defended from all assaults.
Even the legitimate attempt to control pain must always be done with respect for human dignity.

If life and death are to retain their true value, the depths of Christ's sacrifice must be understood, and we must unite ourselves to that sacrifice if we are to hold firm.

PRAYER
Lord Jesus,
who, with supreme dedication,
accepted death on the Cross for our salvation,
grant to us and to all the world's people
a share in your sacrifice on the Cross,
so that what we are and what we do
may always be a free and conscious sharing
in your work of salvation.
To you, O Jesus, Priest and Victim,
honor and glory forever.
R/. Amen.

All: *Our Father...*

Stabat Mater
Make me feel as you have felt;
make my soul to glow and melt
with the love of Christ our Lord.

Eleventh Station
Jesus Is Nailed to the Cross

V/. We adore you, O Christ, and we bless you.
R/. Because by your holy Cross you have redeemed the world.

"They tear holes in my hands and my feet; I can count every one of my bones" (Ps 21:17–18).
The words of the Prophet are fulfilled.
The execution begins.
The torturers' blows crush the hands and feet of the Condemned One against the wood of the Cross.
The nails are driven violently into his wrists. Those nails will hold the condemned man as he hangs in the midst of the inexpressible torments of his agony.
In his body and his supremely sensitive spirit, Christ suffers in a way that goes beyond words.

With him there are crucified two real criminals, one on his right, the other on his left. The prophecy is fulfilled: "He was numbered among the transgressors" (Isa 53:12).

Once the torturers raise the Cross, there will begin an agony that will last three hours. This word too must be fulfilled: "When I am lifted up from the earth, I will draw all people to myself" (Jn 12:32).

62

What is it that "draws" us to the Condemned One who is in agony on the Cross?
Certainly, the sight of such intense suffering stirs compassion. But compassion is not enough to lead us to bind our very life to the One who hangs on the Cross.

How is it that, generation after generation, this appalling sight has drawn countless hosts of people who have made the Cross the hallmark of their faith?
Hosts of men and women who, for centuries, have lived and given their lives looking to this sign?

From the Cross, Christ draws us *by the power of love*,
divine Love, which did not recoil from the total gift of self;
infinite Love, which on the tree of the Cross, raised up from the earth the weight of Christ's body, to counterbalance the weight of the first sin;
boundless Love, which has utterly filled *every* void of love and allowed humanity to find refuge, once more, in the arms of the merciful Father.

May Christ, lifted high on the Cross, draw us, too, the men and women of the new millennium!
In the shadow of the Cross, let us "walk in love, as Christ loved us and gave himself up for us, a fragrant offering and sacrifice to God" (Eph 5:2).

PRAYER
O Christ lifted high,
O Love crucified,
fill our hearts with your love,
that we may see, in your Cross,
the sign of our redemption
and, drawn by your wounds,
we may live and die with you,
who live and reign with the Father and the Spirit,
now and forever.
R/. Amen.

All: *Our Father...*

Stabat Mater
Holy Mother, pierce me through;
in my heart each wound renew
of my Savior crucified.

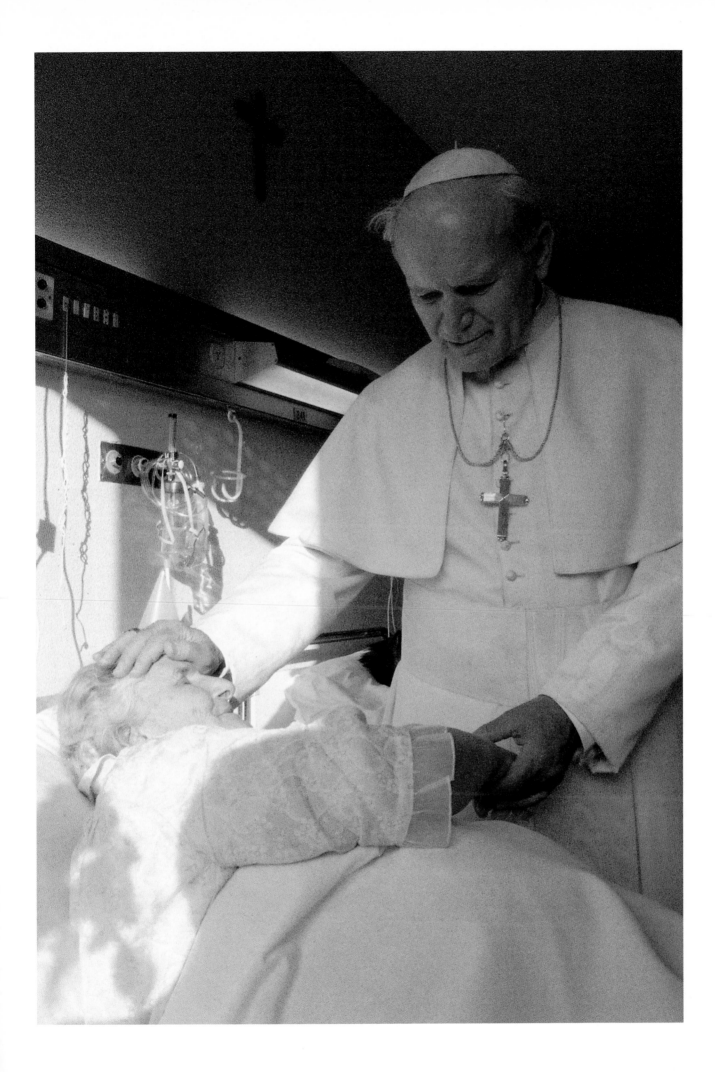

Twelfth Station
Jesus Dies on the Cross

V/. We adore you, O Christ, and we bless you.
R/. Because by your holy Cross you have redeemed the world.

"Father, forgive them, for they know not what they do" (Lk 23:34).
At the height of his Passion, Christ does not forget man, especially those people who are directly responsible for his suffering. Jesus knows that, more than anything else, all human beings need love; they need the mercy which, at this moment, is being poured out into the world.

"Truly, I say to you, today you will be with me in Paradise" (Lk 23:43). This is how Jesus replies to the plea of the criminal hanging on his right: "Jesus, remember me when you come into your kingdom" (Lk 23:42).

The promise of a new life. This is the first fruit of the Passion and imminent Death of Christ. A word of hope to all peoples.

At the foot of the Cross stood Mary, and beside her, the disciple, John the Evangelist. Jesus says: "Woman, behold your son!" and to the disciple: "Behold your mother!" (Jn 19:26–27). And from that moment the disciple took her to his own home" (Jn 19:27).

This is his bequest to those dearest to his heart.
His legacy to the Church.

The desire of Jesus as he dies is that the maternal love of Mary should embrace all those for whom he is giving his life, the whole of humanity.

Immediately after, Jesus cries out: "I am thirsty" (Jn 19:28) This word describes the dreadful burning which consumes his whole body. It is the one word which refers directly to his physical suffering.

Then Jesus adds: "My God, my God, why have you abandoned me?" (Mt 27:46; see Ps 22:2). These words of the Psalm are his prayer. Despite their tone, these words reveal *the depths of his union with the Father*. In the last moments of his life on earth, Jesus thinks of the Father. From this moment on, the dialogue will only be between the dying Son and the Father who accepts his sacrifice of love.

When the ninth hour comes, Jesus cries out: "It is accomplished!" (Jn 19:30).
Now the work of the redemption is complete.
The mission for which he came to earth has reached its fruition.

The rest belongs to the Father:
"Father, into your hands I commit my spirit" (Lk 23:46).
And having said this, he breathed his last.
"The curtain of the temple was torn in two…" (Mt 27:51).
The "Holy of Holies" of the Jerusalem Temple is opened at the moment when it is entered by the Priest of the New and Eternal Covenant.

PRAYER

Lord Jesus Christ,
in the moment of your agony
you were not indifferent to humanity's fate,
and with your last breath
you entrusted to the Father's mercy
the men and women of every age,
with all their weaknesses and sins.
Fill us, and the generations yet to come,
with your Spirit of love,
so that our indifference
will not make the fruits of your death
be given in vain.
To you, crucified Jesus, the wisdom and the power of God,
honor and glory forever and ever.
R/. Amen.

All: *Our Father...*

Stabat Mater
She looked upon her sweet Son,
saw him hang in desolation,
till his spirit forth he sent.

Thirteenth Station
Jesus Is Taken Down From the Cross and Given to His Mother

V/. We adore you, O Christ, and we bless you.
R/. Because by your holy Cross you have redeemed the world.

O quam tristis et afflicta
Fuit illa benedicta
Mater Unigeniti.

In the arms of his Mother they have placed the lifeless body of the Son. The Gospels say nothing of what she felt at that moment.
It is as though, by their silence, the Evangelists wished to respect her sorrow, her feelings, and her memories. Or, that perhaps they simply felt incapable of expressing them.
It is only the devotion of the centuries that has preserved the figure of the "Pietà," providing Christian memory with the most sorrowful image of the ineffable *bond of love* which blossomed in the Mother's heart on the day of the Annunciation and ripened as she waited for the birth of her divine Son.
That love was

revealed in the cave at Bethlehem and was tested already during the Presentation in the Temple. It grew deeper as Mary stored and pondered in her heart all that was happening (see Lk 2:51). Now this intimate bond of love must be transformed into a union which transcends the boundary between life and death.

And thus it will be across the span of the centuries: people pause at Michelangelo's statue of the "Pietà," they kneel before the image of the loving and sorrowful Mother (*Smetna Dobrodziejka*) in the Church of the Franciscans in Krakow, before the Mother of the Seven Sorrows, Patroness of Slovakia, they venerate Our Lady of Sorrows in countless shrines in every part of the world. And so *they learn the difficult love* which does not flee from suffering, but surrenders trustingly to the tenderness of God, for whom nothing is impossible (see Lk 1:37).

PRAYER

Salve, Regina, Mater misericordiæ; vita, dulcedo et spes nostra, salve. Ad te clamamus...illos tuos misericordes oculos ad nos converte et Jesum, benedictum fructum ventris tui, nobis post hoc exilium ostende.
Implore for us the grace of faith, hope and charity, so that we, like you, may stand without flinching beneath the Cross until our last breath.
To your Son, Jesus, our Savior, with the Father and the Holy Spirit, be all honor and glory forever and ever.
R/. Amen.

All: *Our Father...*

Stabat Mater
Let me mingle tears with you,
mourning him who mourned for me,
all the days that I may live.

Fourteenth Station
Jesus Is Laid in the Tomb

V/. We adore you, O Christ, and we bless you.

R/. Because by your holy Cross you have redeemed the world.

"He was crucified, died and was buried...."
The lifeless body of Christ has been laid in the tomb. But the stone of the tomb is not the final seal on his work.
The last word belongs not to falsehood, hatred, and violence.
The last word will be spoken by Love, which is stronger than death.

"Unless a grain of wheat falls into the earth and dies, it remains alone; but if it dies, it bears much fruit" (Jn 12:24).
The tomb is the last stage of Christ's dying through the whole course of his earthly life; *it is the sign of his supreme sacrifice* for us
and for our salvation.

Very soon, this tomb will become *the first proclamation of praise and exaltation of the Son of God in the glory of the Father.*
"He was crucified, died and was buried...on the third day he rose from the dead."

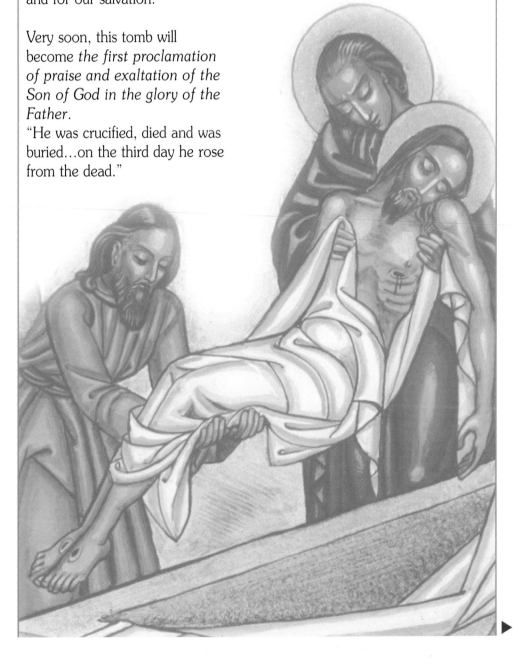

Once the lifeless body of Jesus is laid in the tomb, at the foot of Golgotha, the Church begins the vigil of Holy Saturday.
In the depth of her heart, Mary stores and ponders the Passion of her Son; the women agree to meet on the morning of the day after the Sabbath, in order to anoint Christ's body with aromatic ointments;
the disciples gather in the seclusion of the Upper Room, waiting for the Sabbath to pass.

This vigil will end with the meeting at the tomb, the empty tomb of the Savior.
Then the tomb, the silent witness of the Resurrection, will speak.
The stone rolled back, the inner chamber empty, the cloths on the ground, this will be what John sees when he comes to the tomb with Peter:
"He saw and he believed" (Jn 20:8).
And with him, *the Church believed*,
and from that moment on, she never grows weary of communicating to the world this fundamental truth of her faith:
"Christ has been raised from the dead, the first fruits of those who have fallen asleep" (1 Cor 15:20).

The empty tomb is the sign of the definitive victory
of truth over falsehood,
of good over evil,
of mercy over sin,
of life over death.
The empty tomb is *the sign of the hope* which "does not deceive" (Rom 5:5).
"[Our] hope is full of immortality" (see Wis 3:4).

PRAYER
Lord Jesus Christ,
by the power of the Holy Spirit,
you were drawn by the Father
from the darkness of death
to the light of a new life in glory.
Grant that the sign of the empty tomb
may speak to us and to future generations
and become a well spring of living faith,
generous love,
and unshakable hope.
O you, O Jesus, whose presence, hidden and victorious,
fills the history of the world,
be honor and glory forever and ever.
R/. Amen.

All: *Our Father...*

Stabat Mater
While my body here decays,
may my soul your goodness praise,
safe in paradise with you. Amen.

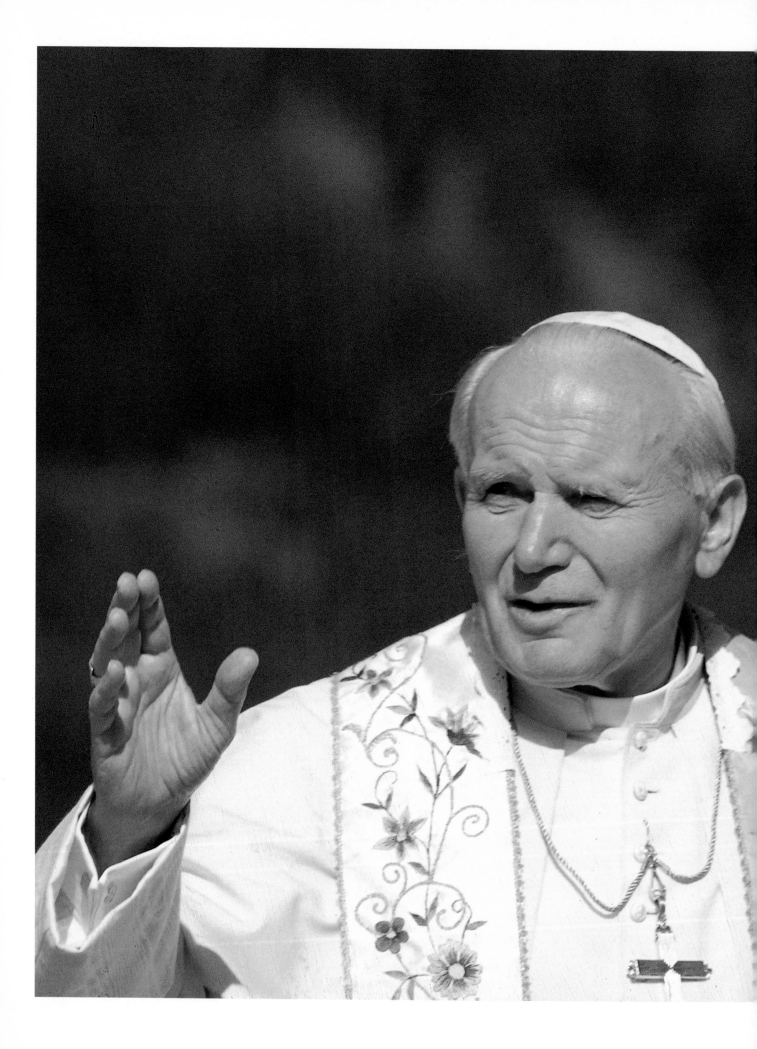

The Holy Father addresses those present.
At the conclusion of his address,
the Holy Father imparts the Apostolic Blessing.

V/. The Lord be with you.
R/. And also with you.

V/. Blessed be the name of the Lord.
R/. Now and forever.

V/. Our help is in the name of the Lord.
R/. Who made heaven and earth.

V/. May Almighty God bless you, the Father,
and the Son, and the Holy Spirit.
R/. Amen.